Tecumseh

History Maker Bios

Susan Bivin Aller

LERNER PUBLICATIONS COMPANY • MINNEAPOLIS

Map on p. 7 by Laura Westlund
Illustrations by Tim Parlin

For the spelling of personal names, groups, and objects, the editors relied on Native American publications and resources. Tecumseh's speeches quoted in this book are translations.

Lerner Publications Company
A division of Lerner Publishing Group
241 First Avenue North
Minneapolis, MN 55401 U.S.A.

Website address: www.lernerbooks.com

Library of Congress Cataloging-in-Publication Data

Aller, Susan Bivin.
    Tecumseh / by Susan Bivin Aller.
        p.   cm. — (History maker bios)
    Summary: A biography of Tecumseh, whose integrity, personal magnetism, and public speaking skills helped him to lead the Shawnee and people of other tribes in the fight to save their lives and lands from being taken by white men. Includes bibliographical references and index.
    ISBN: 0–8225–0699–8 (lib. bdg. : alk. paper)
    1. Tecumseh, Shawnee chief, 1768–1813—Juvenile literature. 2. Shawnee Indians—Biography—Juvenile literature. [1. Tecumseh, Shawnee chief, 1768–1813. 2. Shawnee Indians—Biography. 3. Indians of North America—East (U.S.)—Biography. 4. Kings, queens, rulers, etc.] I. Title. II. Series.
    E99.S35T1125 2004
    977'.004973'0092—dc21   2003009053

Manufactured in the United States of America
1 2 3 4 5 6 – JR – 09 08 07 06 05 04

TABLE OF CONTENTS

INTRODUCTION

The Shawnee hero Tecumseh has been called one of the greatest Native American leaders.

Tecumseh's battleground was the American frontier in the late 1700s and early 1800s. As white settlers moved west, Tecumseh fought to keep land from being taken away from Native Americans.

Native Americans admired him for trying to save their homes from white settlers. Whites feared him because his army of Native Americans was prepared to fight to the death. But Tecumseh's friends and enemies alike agreed that he was an extraordinary man.

This is his story.

1 SHOOTING STAR

A bright meteor streaked across the sky on a cold March night in 1768. Inside a bark-covered house on the banks of a river, a Shawnee mother gave birth to her fourth child, a son. She named him Tecumseh, Shawnee for "shooting star."

Tecumseh was born in what became southern Ohio. Long before Ohio, Michigan, Indiana, Illinois, Wisconsin, and Minnesota became states, these lands had been home to generations of Native Americans. They fished in the rivers, hunted in the woods, and farmed the land. But to white people living in the East, this land was a frontier to be explored. And they wanted its rivers, woods, and farmland for themselves. They called it the Northwest Territory.

Northwest Territory

MINNESOTA

Lake Superior

CANADA

WISCONSIN

Lake Michigan

Lake Huron

BATTLE OF THE THAMES

Lake Ontario

MICHIGAN

Fort Detroit ■ ×

Lake Erie

N

Fort Dearborn ■

Maumee River

Tippecanoe River

BATTLE OF TIPPECANOE ×●

Prophets-town

■—Fort Wayne

BATTLE OF FALLEN TIMBERS ×

ILLINOIS

INDIANA

OHIO

Ohio River

Wabash River

Miles
0   50   100   150

0   50 100 150 200
Kilometers

Tecumseh's father Pukeshinwau was a war chief of the Kispoko band of Shawnees. One day, six-year-old Tecumseh watched his father and oldest brother prepare to join a great war party. Big Knives—white soldiers from Virginia—were marching toward Tecumseh's village. The Shawnee war party was going out to stop them.

SACRED LANDS

The Shawnees believed there were spirits in all living things—in animals, in the rain and wind, in the stars, sun, and moon. The land itself was a gift of the Great Spirit. The Shawnees spent much time and effort in pleasing these spirits. If the spirits were angry, crops would not grow, animals needed for food would disappear, and there would be sickness and death.

In fall and spring, the Shawnees held days of feasting, dancing, and games. They thanked the spirits for good hunting and harvests and prayed for the success of new crops.

Shawnees used weapons like this tomahawk in battle.

The Big Knives said they had bought the land from the Shawnees. They demanded that the Shawnees leave. Pukeshinwau said the Shawnees had not sold their land. To the Shawnees, the land along the Ohio River was a sacred place given to them by their Great Spirit. They would never sell it.

Tecumseh watched the warriors pray to the spirits for protection. They painted their bodies and shaved their heads except for a long lock of hair on top. Then they danced to a pounding drum, faster and faster. The war chief began to sing a war song. The men fired their guns into the air and shouted as they followed him from the village.

Shawnee war chief Cornstalk led the attack at Point Pleasant in 1774.

The Shawnees attacked the soldiers at Point Pleasant, West Virginia, on October 10, 1774. They fought fiercely, but there were too many Big Knives. Many Shawnees were killed, including Tecumseh's father.

Tecumseh's mother, Methoatasskee, faced a difficult time. She already had five children and was expecting again soon. That winter, Methoatasskee gave birth to triplets. She did her best to raise her family, including the bright and mischievous Tecumseh.

Tecumseh's mother could not protect her children from what was coming. In 1775, the American colonies declared they wanted to be free from British rule. A great war, the American Revolution, began. Great Britain wanted the help of Native Americans, who were armed and trained in warfare. The American colonists wanted the native peoples' help too.

The American Revolution began in Massachusetts in 1775. Native American warriors fought on both sides.

Some Shawnees wanted to stay out of the war. Others thought that if they fought with the winning side, they would be allowed to keep their land after the war. Tecumseh's band, the Kispoko, sided with the British. But there was a high price to pay. Tecumseh's family had to escape five times when American colonists burned their villages.

Wampum belts were used between Native American groups to send messages of peace or war.

After the American Revolution ended in 1783, many Native Americans were forced or bribed to turn over their land to the new U.S. government. The government gave Native American land to soldiers as a reward for their service. It sold other land to companies, which then sold pieces to white settlers.

Tecumseh's people refused to give up their villages and the places where they hunted and fished. As a tide of white settlement swept toward them, the Shawnees continued to fight to save their lands.

2 BOLD WARRIOR

As Tecumseh grew, his oldest brother, Cheeseekau, taught him the skills needed to be a warrior. Tecumseh became an expert in tracking and shooting animals for food. One day, he shot sixteen buffalo with arrows as he sat in a tree above a stampeding herd.

Tecumseh learned stories of the Shawnees' beginnings. The Shawnees believed they were the Great Spirit's favorite people. The Great Spirit had given them land along the Ohio River. As long as the Shawnees lived in their sacred homeland, their creator would bless them.

VISION QUESTS

Like all Shawnee boys, Tecumseh went on a vision quest when he was about fourteen. The vision quest helped a boy find his own personal guardian spirit. He went alone into the woods. He did not eat and spent his time meditating.

After fasting and meditating, the boy's guardian spirit came to him, perhaps in a dream or trance. The spirit might appear as an animal or bird. The boy was the only one who knew what it was, and he was forbidden to tell anyone. The spirit gave protection and strength to the boy throughout his life.

Young Tecumseh learned to tell stories in picture writing. He also learned to make speeches and found he had a special gift for it. As he grew older, Tecumseh's speeches became his most powerful weapons.

Tecumseh grew to be tall, strong, and handsome. He was friendly and generous, and he liked to laugh. At festivals, he danced and played games. People in the band liked the high-spirited boy. Girls flirted with him, and he flirted back. But Tecumseh had a serious side. His goal in life was to become a Shawnee warrior like his father.

As a young man, Tecumseh became famous for his hunting skills.

Hundreds of flatboats carrying white settlers came down the Ohio River.

Like his father, Tecumseh wanted to stop the white settlers who traveled down the Ohio River to claim Native American lands. The settlers said the Native Americans had signed away their land in treaties, or agreements.

But the Shawnees and other nations said the treaties were no good. They warned the settlers to stop. Still, flatboats by the hundreds came down the river. Young Tecumseh and his fellow warriors ambushed the boats, looted the goods, and took some of the settlers prisoner.

When Tecumseh was about twenty-one, his brother Cheeseekau led the family and some followers to Tennessee. On the way, Tecumseh was thrown from his horse. The accident shattered his thighbone. He was afraid he would be crippled. Tecumseh did not want to live if he could not be a warrior. After many months, his leg healed, but he limped slightly for the rest of his life.

In Tennessee, Tecumseh's family lived with their friends, a Cherokee band called the Chickamaugas. They were fierce raiders like the Shawnees.

Blue Jacket (CENTER) led one thousand warriors to victory over General St. Clair's army at the Wabash River.

General Arthur St. Clair was an American soldier born in Scotland.

Tecumseh stayed in Tennessee for about two years. During that time, he had a daughter with a Cherokee woman. In 1791, he returned to Ohio to help hold the line against the advancing Americans.

A major battle took place at the Wabash River in November 1791. One thousand warriors from several nations, including Shawnee and Miami, destroyed an army led by General Arthur St. Clair. Settlers and land companies panicked at the fierce attack. For a while, white settlers stopped moving into Native American land.

Cheeseekau was still in Tennessee. He boldly organized raids on new white settlements growing along the Cumberland River. He sent for Tecumseh to help. One September night, the raiders were advancing toward a fort under a full moon. A soldier guarding the fort saw them and fired a single shot. Cheeseekau was killed instantly.

Tecumseh grieved for Cheeseekau. He had even more reason to hate the white soldiers. They had killed both his father and brother.

Tecumseh was only twenty-four years old, but his hunting skills and his bravery in battle had already made him famous. People were attracted by his strong personality. They felt his guardian spirit must be very powerful. When Tecumseh spoke, his dramatic words moved people to action. "War or extermination is now our only choice," he told his fellow Shawnees. "Which do you choose?"

3 A DREAM OF UNITY

Tecumseh took part in a great assembly of Native American leaders held in Ohio in 1792. Hundreds came from as far away as Canada and Florida— Wyandot, Ottawa, Ojibwa, Potawatomi, Sauk, Delaware, Fox, Creek, and Cherokee. They passed around a pipe and smoked it to show their goodwill.

Native Americans shared a pipe like this to show they wanted to live peacefully with each other.

Tecumseh challenged the leaders. They must stand united, he argued. They must fight each other's battles and help destroy each other's enemies.

The U.S. government was powerful. If it had to fight for the land, it would fight to win. But the government did not want an expensive war with great loss of life on both sides. There were thousands of settlers on their way west. The government wanted to open up Native American lands for these white pioneers without having to resort to violence. It hoped it could buy the land with money and goods, such as knives, guns, tools, and cloth.

The U.S. government and the Native American assembly tried peace talks, but they failed. Neither side could come up with a plan that made both sides happy. A battle lay ahead.

MOVING WEST

After the American Revolution, even more white settlers began to move west. The U.S. government wanted to make the country bigger. It encouraged explorers and settlers to move to the territories. If more white people lived in the territories, the territories could become states.

But Native Americans already lived in these territories, and their way of life was different. Native Americans hunted over huge areas of common land. The U.S. government believed that if Native Americans settled down and became farmers, they would not need hunting grounds. They would sell their land to the government.

In 1794, U.S. Army general Anthony Wayne led five thousand infantry and cavalry troops into Ohio. The Native Americans had only about 1,500 warriors. Tecumseh and the other Native Americans hoped for help from their old allies the British. The British still had forts in the area. But the British did not want to take sides and refused to help. In August, the Native Americans fought alone against the U.S. Army at the Battle of Fallen Timbers on the Maumee River in Ohio.

Native Americans helped the British hold Fort Detroit until 1796.

Shawnee, Miami, Ojibwa, and Delaware fought against the U.S. Army at Fallen Timbers.

General Wayne's army defeated the Native Americans. Families were forced to leave behind their crops and villages. About one thousand men, women, and children spent a miserable winter suffering in the cold and living off food begged from the British. Tecumseh was one of them.

General Wayne prepared a peace treaty for the chiefs to sign. The treaty was written on parchment paper seven feet long and three feet wide. It gave the United States nearly all of present-day Ohio, part of Indiana, and places that became Detroit, Toledo, and Chicago. Eleven hundred chiefs signed it. But Tecumseh, angry and discouraged, refused.

General Anthony Wayne's Treaty of Greenville was signed in Ohio on August 5, 1795.

Tecumseh felt helpless against the growing number of white settlers and soldiers. His dream of an alliance of nations was dying. In 1797, he led his followers to Indiana. Other Native Americans who looked to Tecumseh for leadership joined him.

In 1800, U.S. president Thomas Jefferson appointed William Henry Harrison governor of the Indiana Territory. Jefferson encouraged Harrison to do all he could to acquire Native American lands. At twenty-seven, Harrison was an ambitious soldier and politician. He had fought in several battles against Native Americans, including Fallen Timbers. Harrison knew that if he did well as governor, he might become an even more important public official.

Tecumseh and Harrison were on a collision course.

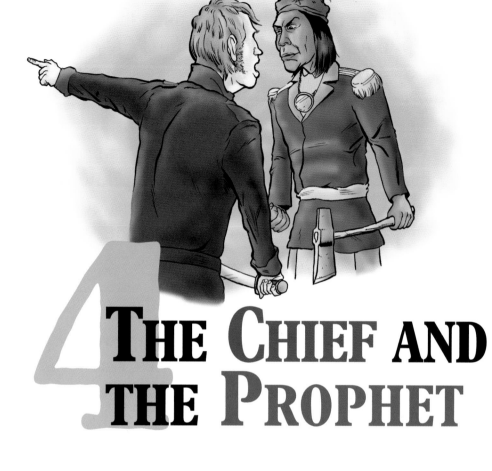

4 THE CHIEF AND THE PROPHET

During the winter of 1804–1805, the Shawnees faced starvation and disease. Floods had damaged their crops, so they had almost nothing to eat. Deadly diseases carried by the white settlers swept through villages and killed hundreds of Native Americans.

White men also gave whiskey to the Native Americans, knowing that it would make them weak and sick. The Native Americans began to trade their lands for whiskey.

The Native Americans were fighting for survival. They believed they must have done something terrible for which their Great Spirit was punishing them. During this sad period, Tecumseh's youngest brother, Tenskwatawa, had a vision. The Great Spirit showed Tenskwatawa how the Native Americans were being destroyed by contact with white people. They must return to the Native American way of life.

Tenskwatawa's name in Shawnee means "the open door."

Tenskwatawa began to tell people about his vision. His powerful preaching inspired Native Americans all through the territory. He became known as the Prophet.

Tecumseh and Tenskwatawa built a new village where the Tippecanoe and Wabash Rivers met in Indiana. They called it Prophetstown. No whiskey was allowed there. Only traditional Native American religion could be practiced. There was no talk of war.

The Wabash River is seen from a path called Tecumseh's Trail.

A white soldier once described Tecumseh as "one of the finest looking men I ever saw."

Prophetstown became a religious center where Native Americans reformed their lives and worshiped the Great Spirit. Shawnee, Wyandot, Delaware, Ottawa, Kickapoo, and Ojibwa people moved to Prophetstown to share in its spirit. Others came from far away just to hear the Prophet speak.

The Prophet's teachings gave new life to Tecumseh's hopes for a union of Native American nations. Tecumseh traveled from the Great Lakes to the Gulf of Mexico forging alliances with many leaders.

Governor Harrison became alarmed
when he heard what Tecumseh was doing.
He called eleven minor chiefs together at
Fort Wayne in Indiana and had them sign a
treaty. The treaty gave three million acres
of Native American land to the
government's Indiana Territory. But the
eleven chiefs had no authority to give this
land away. Dishonest Potawatomi chiefs
signed away Shawnee lands. Others also
signed away land they didn't own.

Tecumseh was outraged. Governor Harrison offered to hear Tecumseh's complaints. In August 1810, eighty canoes filled with Native Americans swept down the Wabash River to meet the governor.

The meeting between Tecumseh and Harrison was tense. They met on the grounds of Harrison's house, in a clearing in a grove of trees. Tecumseh spoke first, starting slowly and then talking with more speed and passion.

WILLIAM HENRY HARRISON

William Henry Harrison was a soldier, governor, diplomat, and eventually president of the United States. But it was in the early frontier battles in the Indiana Territory that Harrison and Tecumseh crossed paths.

Harrison feared and respected Tecumseh. He called Tecumseh "one of those uncommon geniuses which spring up occasionally to . . . overturn the established order of things."

He told Harrison that no Native American had the right to sell land that belonged to all the native peoples together. "Sell a country!" he said. "Why not sell the air, the clouds and the great sea, as well as the earth? Did not the Great Spirit make them all for the use of his children?"

Harrison could not see Tecumseh's side of the argument. The treaties were fair, he said. Tecumseh lost his temper. As he rose to his feet, his warriors also rose, fingering their war clubs. Tecumseh called Harrison a liar. Harrison drew his sword, and his soldiers moved forward.

Then Harrison took control of the situation by announcing that the meeting was over. He would reply to the Native Americans' complaints in writing. Tecumseh and his warriors left. There had been no bloodshed. But Tecumseh saw that a war between the Native Americans and white Americans was certain to come. He would be ready.

5 LIKE A HERO GOING HOME

Seeing a war coming, Tecumseh quickly gathered support. In six months, he traveled Native American lands from New York to the Great Lakes, across the Midwest and into the South. The powerful Creek nation in Georgia and Florida joined Tecumseh's alliance.

Word of Tecumseh's growing union of nations reached Governor Harrison. The governor had ambitions to govern more than a territory. He wanted statehood for Indiana. But Harrison saw that he would first have to get rid of Tecumseh and the people he considered savages.

Harrison decided to strike Tecumseh's village and followers while Tecumseh was traveling. In November 1811, Harrison sent nine hundred soldiers to Prophetstown. The Native Americans attacked first. But when they ran out of ammunition, they had to retreat. Harrison claimed victory in what became known as the Battle of Tippecanoe.

The Native Americans lost the Battle of Tippecanoe, but many U.S. soldiers were killed and wounded.

William Henry Harrison built Fort Harrison in Indiana in 1811.

Tecumseh returned to find his village in ruins. All the buildings had been burned. Reserves of food and ammunition were destroyed. Tecumseh's brother the Prophet was in disgrace for failing to save the village. A terrible winter lay ahead for Tecumseh's people. They had nowhere to live and nothing to eat. They were forced to take shelter with nearby Wyandot people.

Tecumseh's dream of an alliance of nations ended with the Battle of Tippecanoe. In its place came a nightmare of border wars and raids on white settlements. Native Americans wanted revenge for Tippecanoe. Tecumseh could not stop them. Fearing for their lives, settlers abandoned their homes.

37

Many battles during the War of 1812 were fought at sea or on the Great Lakes.

The U.S. government believed that the British were encouraging the Native American raids. The United States wanted to force Great Britain out of the Northwest Territory and declared war. It became known as the War of 1812.

Tecumseh decided to help the British fight the Americans. He offered them a military force of Shawnee, Kickapoo, Delaware, Sioux, Winnebago, and Sauk. Tecumseh fought and won several major battles of the war, including one at Fort Detroit in Michigan.

Then a U.S. naval force, led by Commodore Oliver Perry, captured the small British fleet on Lake Erie. This cut off British supply lines.

The war turned in favor of the United States. Meanwhile, a massive army of Kentucky volunteers was pressing toward the field of battle. Its commander was William Henry Harrison, Tecumseh's enemy.

Tecumseh expected the British to fight alongside his warriors against Harrison's forces. But the British commander, General Henry Proctor, planned to retreat into Canada to make a stand there. Tecumseh insisted on meeting with Proctor. When he rose to speak, surrounded by his warriors, Tecumseh made a magnificent figure. A deerskin suit showed off his tall, muscular figure. He wore a plume of white feathers in his headband. One observer said he had a "singularly wild and terrific expression. . . . It was evident that he could be terrible."

During the Battle of Lake Erie, Oliver Perry rowed to a ship to save it from the British.

Tecumseh and Henry Proctor argued over the best way to fight the U.S. Army.

Tecumseh lashed out at Proctor. "You always told us to remain here and take care of our lands. . . . But now, Father [Proctor], we see you are drawing back. . . . We must compare our father's conduct to a fat dog that carries its tail upon its back, but when affrighted, it drops it between its legs and runs off."

Tecumseh did not want to leave his homeland. He feared he might never return. But he could not fight alone against Harrison's huge army. Filled with anger and despair, he followed Proctor into Canada.

The combined Native American and British forces made their stand in a marshy, wooded area on the north bank of the Thames River in Ontario. The British soldiers were in bad shape after marching for days. They had lost much of their ammunition. They were cold, hungry, and discouraged. It was Tecumseh, not General Proctor, who rallied the British soldiers before the Battle of the Thames. Moving along the line of men, he pressed their hands and tried to encourage them.

When it comes your time to die, sing your death song and die like a hero going home. —Tecumseh

No one knows exactly how Tecumseh died at the Battle of the Thames.

On October 5, 1813, the combined Native American and British forces of about one thousand faced Harrison's army of 3,500. As the U.S. soldiers made their first charge and scattered the British line, Proctor abandoned his men and galloped away.

With Proctor gone, Tecumseh was in command. The men heard him shouting through the noise of the battle. "Tell your young men to stand firm. . . . Have a big heart!" Through the smoke, they saw him standing alone, his face war-painted black and red, firing his musket. Then, suddenly, they saw him no more.

When his warriors realized that Tecumseh was dead, they lost heart. With loud yells of grief, they left the battlefield.

"Our lives are in the hands of the Great Spirit," he had told his army. "We are determined to defend our lands, and if it is his will, we wish to leave our bones upon them."

Tecumseh showed courage, vision, and inspiration. He brought many Native Americans together into an armed resistance movement. And he fought to the death to preserve his people's sacred homelands.

AFTER TECUMSEH

The Battle of the Thames ended the Native Americans' hopes of holding onto the Northwest Territory. No other leader could match Tecumseh's skill in keeping people united. "Since our great Tecumseh is killed," one chief said sadly, "we do not listen to one another." More than one thousand of Tecumseh's followers spent the next few years near starvation at the head of Lake Ontario.

TIMELINE

In the year . . .

1774	Tecumseh's father is killed in the battle at Point Pleasant, West Virginia.	Age 6
1775	the American Revolution began.	
1789	he and his family move to Tennessee.	Age 21
1792	his brother Cheeseekau is killed. he attends a large assembly of Native American leaders in Ohio.	
1794	he fights against the U.S. Army in the Battle of Fallen Timbers in Ohio.	Age 26
1797	he leads his followers to the White River in Indiana.	
1800	Thomas Jefferson is elected president of the United States. William Henry Harrison is appointed governor of the Indiana Territory.	
1803	the Louisiana Territory is purchased.	
1805	his brother Tenskwatawa has a religious vision. Together they establish a village and call it Prophetstown.	Age 37
1810	he meets with Governor Harrison in Indiana, but they part in anger.	
1811	the Battle of Tippecanoe is fought. Prophetstown is destroyed.	
1812	the War of 1812 begins. he leads Native American warriors in the Fall of Fort Detroit.	
1813	he dies in the Battle of the Thames in Canada.	Age 45

MODERN SHAWNEES

After Tecumseh's death in the War of 1812, the Shawnees separated into smaller bands and went to live in various parts of the country. War and disease killed large numbers of them. But in the 1900s their numbers increased to many thousands. Four large groups of Shawnees live in Oklahoma, Missouri, and Ohio. They are the Absentee Tribe, the Cherokee Nation as Adopted Shawnees, the Eastern Shawnee Tribe, and the Shawnee Tribe of Miami, Oklahoma. In all the groups, Tecumseh is honored as a hero.

This marble statue, called "The Dying Tecumseh," once stood in the U.S. Capitol.

FURTHER READING

NONFICTION

Connell, Kate. *These Lands Are Ours: Tecumseh's Fight for the Old Northwest.* Austin, TX: Raintree/Steck-Vaughn, 1993. The story of Tecumseh's bravery on behalf of his people.

Mattern, Joanne. *The Shawnee Indians.* Mankato, MN: Bridgestone Books, 2001. Color photographs and maps illustrate the story of the Shawnee, from history to the present day.

Schmittroth, Linda. *Shawnee.* Woodbridge, CT: Blackbirch Press, 2002. An illustrated account of Shawnee history, culture, and daily life.

FICTION

Alder, Elizabeth. *Crossing the Panther's Path.* New York: Farrar, Straus & Giroux, 2002. A novel based on the true story of Billy Calder, the teenager who volunteered to be Tecumseh's translator and aide during the War of 1812.

WEBSITES

James Madison University
<http:www.jmu.edu/madison/tecumseh> The university's website features a link to Tecumseh.

Ohio History Central
<http://www.ohiohistorycentral.org> This website features links to the history and culture of Ohio Native Americans, with maps and historic images of battles and people.

Old Northwest Historical Society
<http://home.fuse.net/rrowan> This website dedicated to early frontier history features links to the Tippecanoe, Fallen Timbers, and Vincennes battlefield websites.

The Shawnee Tribe
<http://www.shawnee-tribe.org> The official website of the Shawnee tribe provides information on the Shawnee government, events, and education. There are also sections on Shawnee culture, history, and language, and a gallery of photos and paintings.

Select Bibliography

Blaisdell, Bob, ed. *Great Speeches by Native Americans.* Mineola, N.Y.: Dover Publications, 2000.

Josephy Jr., Alvin M. *The Patriot Chiefs.* New York: Viking Press, 1961.

Nies, Judith. *Native American History.* New York: Ballantine Books, 1996.

Sugden, John. *Tecumseh: A Life.* New York: Henry Holt, 1997.

INDEX

For photographs and artwork: Ohio Historical Society, pp. 4, 10, 12, 18, 25, 26, 31; © Bettmann/CORBIS, pp. 9, 11, 17, 36, 40; Library of Congress, LC USZ62-19459, p. 16; © Stapleton Collection/CORBIS, p. 19; © Geoffrey Clements/CORBIS, p. 22; Burton Historical Collection, Detroit Public Library, p. 24; © Hulton|Archive by Getty Images, pp. 29, 37, 38, 42; Library of Congress, LC-D4-14802, p. 30; Library of Congress, LC USZ62-416663-13009, p. 32; Library of Congress, LC-D416-14221, p. 39; Smithsonian American Art Museum, Washington, DC/Art Resource, NY, p. 45. Front cover, © Bettmann/CORBIS. Back cover, Ohio Historical Society.
For quoted material: p. 20, Blaisdell, Bob, ed. *Great Speeches by Native Americans.* Mineola, NY: Dover Publications, 2000; p. 41, "An American Hero: Tecumseh," James Madison University <http://www.jmu.edu/madison/tecumseh>; pp. 31, 33, 34, 39, 40, 42, 43, Sugden, John. *Tecumseh.* New York: Henry Holt, 1997.